In The Room
An Actor's Guide To Auditioning

Pedro Miguel Arce

Published by Dancing Sumo Productions
www.dancingsumo.com

Cover Design: P.M. Arce
Book Layout: P.M. Arce
Editor: Alexis Fakouri

ISBN-10: 0989884309
ISBN-13: 978-0-9898843-0-3

DEDICATION

For Earl my own personal Yoda.

CONTENTS

ACKNOWLEDGMENTS

I would like to thank all my friends and colleagues who have helped me, not only putting this book together but through out my career. Special thanks to Alexis for your help and guidance, Ashley and Kate for your input, Olga for your support. A special thank you to my mother..

INTRODUCTION

Pedro Miguel Arce has appeared in over a dozen feature films like; George A. Romero's Land Of The Dead, Get Rich Or Die Trying, Are We Done Yet, Please Kill Mr. Know It All, and most recently, Mortal Instruments - City of Bones, 20 television commercials including: A&W, Dell Computers, Labatt's Blue, Kudo, 3 Mobil (Asia) Poker Lotto and Mitsubishi, and over 20 TV shows including How I met Your Mother, CSI:Miami, Las Vegas, Flashpoint, Lost Girl, and Warehouse 13. A complete list can be found on www.IMDB.com.

Pedro honed his acting skills by training in Los Angeles at the Berg Institute, in Toronto with EVN Studios and also trained in The Second City where he developed some of his improvisation skills.

Pedro has walked into many an audition room in Los Angeles, Toronto, Vancouver, and Montreal , and booked the job. He has also submitted self-tapes, and has even booked a couple auditions via Skype.

Recently Pedro started working on the other side of the camera as a producer and director. While holding auditions for a project he was directing, Pedro was amazed by how ill prepared some of the actors were in their readings, so he decided to write this book to help fellow actors learn a thing or two about going into the room.

..

PREFACE

This guide is not intended to teach you HOW to act but it is a tool to guide you through the audition process.

I am assuming that you have some **acting chops.**

I am assuming that you know how to act, that you have some training, and that you simply didn't wake up one day and decide to call yourself an actor. This book will not help you *get* auditions for movies, TV, commercials, or even agents. It will guide you through the audition itself ….and may very well help you book the job.

I cannot make you a talented artist, that part's all you, but we know this business is not based on talent alone; I will give you some hints on little things you can do once you get in the room (and leading up to it) that can separate you from the amateurs.

Through out this guide you will find terms that have been underlined and in bold. These are terms that I feel may need some further clarification as to how they are used in the **Biz**. You can find these terms in the Glossary at the end of the book.

THE CALL

You got the call, or more and more commonly, the email, saying that you have an audition with so-and-so Casting Director. You're excited. In my opinion this is where the audition process begins. Once I get that audition notice, I immediately put myself "**IN THE ROOM**."

At this point I recommend you to *be grateful*; give thanks to whatever higher power you asked to help get you the audition in the first place. Some people thank God, some the universe, and some just thank their agents. I say you should just thank them all, (hey - It can't hurt.) Personally, I like to close my eyes and just say, "Thank You" out loud (… but not too loud… or people will talk.)

Now its time for a little checklist I like to make:
1. Check that the **sides** are attached to the email.
2. Check that you are able to open the file for the sides.
3. Check that they are the right sides for your **character**.
4. Check to see that the address for your audition is in the email.
5. Check to make sure that the date and time is in there too.
6. Check to make sure there is a **breakdown** attached.

Tiny details? Yes. Yet still, very important.

If all of these check out, make sure to *send a confirmation Email* to your agent or to whoever sent you the audition notice.

THE BREAKDOWN

I always like to do some research on the people working on the project, so I take look at the breakdown and see what other shows that casting director has worked on. I do this on www.IMDB.com. I always check to see if I have worked with them in the past. Then I do the same for the writer, producers and finally the director. By looking up the director's work I can get a feel for the type of work they do…and therefore what they may like and possibly expect.

If it is a TV series, then I try to watch an episode or two if it's available, for this I turn to the network that puts on the show or Netflix. Some shows have a totally different feel than others. YouTube is always a safe bet for at least a clip or two of the show you are going in to read for. There is always a little something that you will pick up by watching an episode of a show knowing that you are going in to read for it. If you are new to the Biz and are auditioning for short films by new directors they might not have much, if any previous work, but it is still worth a look.

Watching it will give you a sense of the rhythm and timing of the writing and actors. I once had an audition for a show that was known for its fast paced witty banter between the characters. I had never seen the show before, but when a friend of mine found out I was reading for it he made me watch an episode to help me see me just how fast they speak. This information was very helpful to me, even though the Casting Director told me just before the audition that all the characters in the show speak very fast, had I not known this before coming in the room the new note might have thrown me off. Fortunately I was able prepare for that ahead of time - thanks to having watched an episode of the show.

THE SIDES

Chances are that you will not get the whole script, unless you are reading for a **series regular.** What you will get are sides. Sides are the pages of the script where your character appears in the show. Sometimes you will have three or more scenes so the sides will be broken up to only the pages they want to see you do. Whether you print them or read them off a screen somewhere. Do that; READ them. Read the whole thing a few times over. Before you start "playing" the part, **read the scenes and** *understand* **them**.

I love my iPad and often learn my lines on it, but I do like to print the sides to take them in the room with me. I print two sets. I highlight all my lines in green on one set, and the other set I highlight all the lines that the other person says, this will help your scene partner. You may laugh at me for this but I like to highlight my lines in green because it's the color of money. And as much as I love my craft, I do act to pay my bills… it is my career. I am blessed to do what I love for a living.

Know the scene. I know I said this is not a book on acting technique, but I must make this clear. *You have to understand the scene*. Do **the work**. Mess up the paper and mark it up with your thoughts, your inner dialog and as much as I hate the term - your "inspiration" in the scene. Once you know the scene and know what you want in it, the lines will come naturally. The words on the page will become the only thing that would make sense to say at the time.

There are tools that you can use to help you learn your lines. As I mentioned, I like to use my iPad. There is one tool that I find to be extremely useful and that is *Rehearsal 2*; it is a great app that will let you download the script to your device. It lets you highlight the dialog, mark up the script, and lets you black out your lines to help you memorize them. You can even record yourself reading the scene so you can listen to it and it also lets you record notes. It is a great little tool. But if you're less technologically inclined, the paper in front of you is enough.

I like to memorize chunks of the script at a time and I let the chunks get larger as I go. Whenever I do screw up the lines I always go back to the top and start over. I do find that the best thing for learning your lines is to do the scene over and over again.

Normally you get the audition notice a day or two before. I like to get to working on it as soon as possible. If it is the day before I like to do the work early and let it sink in to my head. I will read it over again a couple times before bed and I take the sides to bed with me. I like to read it first thing in the morning as well, just to make sure that it's fresh in my brain.

THE HELP

Get a friend to help you with your audition, preferably a fellow actor. Working with a fellow actor is good for a couple reasons:

1 - Another actor will know a little more about the acting part and may give you notes on what you're doing. And more importantly:

2 - Another actor will be more likely to do it without complaining about having to help you because they will need your help with their audition at some point.

<u>It is extremely important to practice the scene with someone else so that when you get in the room it's not your first time doing the scene out loud with a partner.</u>

Once you have your partner go over the scene, then go over it again. Do it until you are **off page**. BUT stop before you get bored of it and play it out too much. It is difficult to find this balance, trust your gut with this and stop when you feel you're ready. Like everything else this will come easier with practice.

Sometimes there might be something that you just did not catch. It could be something small but very important. I remember working with a good friend of mine who happens to be a very talented actor, I had prepared the sides for my read, I was ready to go but I was early for the audition so I went by her place before with a couple of coffees. She suggested we run the scene. I ran it with her once and she looked a little confused. She read the sides over again. She looked at the name of the show; it was a **pilot** so there wasn't any info on it online. She said that another friend of hers read for a different part. Then she said the one thing that changed my whole read, "you know this is a comedy, right?."

I didn't.

We ran it a few times and it eventually got funny. Thankfully.

THE WARDROBE

Once upon a time, I used to dress exactly like the part I was going in for. I even went as far as getting a make-up artist friend of mine to give me a bald cap and I let my pony tail out from it… I was going in as a Genie. It was a huge spot, I think it was a national car commercial. I was excited. I walked in looking more like a genie than anyone else in that room. I thought for sure this was my spot. Well…the look on the casting director's face when I walked in that room changed my mind about that real fast. The casting director looked at me and I looked at him and I am sure he wanted to either laugh, cry, or yell at me. He just shook his head. I shrugged it off and did my thing. All he could focus on was my head. It was more of a distraction to them, than anything. Guess what- I didn't get it.

On another spot I was going in as Genghis Khan, this time, I didn't go quite so far but I did buy a fur coat from Goodwill and made it into a vest. (I used staples to put it together) This attempt was different; it got a more positive reception from the people in the waiting room. The casting assistant smiled at me when she saw the vest, I smiled back and I was excited to show her the rest of my costume… I pulled from my bag , two machetes that I was going to do some fancy sword play with to impress the casting director with my martial arts prowess. Her smile quickly faded and said to me, "Do not even think about taking those things in there." It was a great note from her. I booked that spot. It was my first commercial job ever.

The lesson here: Give a *hint of the character* but **don't dress the part**, unless it is requested. If they ask you to wear a suit then wear one. If they ask for shorts wear them, most likely they need to see your legs. If they want you to go in as a cop it may be enough to just show up in a button up shirt, and slacks. No toy gun. And whatever you do, don't dress up like a Genie.

BONUS HINT:

It may seem like a no-brainer but a good meal is important before your audition. Have something nutritious, that will give you energy – but isn't too heavy. A couple times I've gone into auditions without having eaten anything and have gotten really light-headed and I didn't give my best audition. Get some fuel in you before you go in the room.

THE HEADSHOT / RESUME

The Internet has saved many trees in this regard. I find that more and more casting directors do not need to get your headshot resume, since they have all of your information online. BUT always have a couple ready for them. Even if you can email them one from your smart phone always have a headshot/resume available for them to see. I recently had an audition where the Casting Director asked me for a resume, I gave her one and it turns out that one I pulled out was not stapled together. I tried to take it back and she said, "no, it's a good thing we are in an office." Then she picked up a stapler and stapled my picture and resume together. It may seem like a small thing but I felt like I was not prepared and it frankly it embarrassed me a little. Luckily I ended up having a good read, so I walked out thinking about the read and not the staples.

These headshots are your calling cards make sure they look professional. I remember helping a friend of mine with a casting session, I was operating the camera and reading with the actors. When we were packing up at the end of the day, as she was putting all the headshots together there were two that stood out, literally. One of the Headshots was a photocopy of her headshot with a resume stapled to the back of it but it was not cut to the proper size, it was still the normal paper size 8.5 by 11 inches. The other one was also an 8.5 by 11 resume but the picture was a small post card size picture of the actor. My director friend looked at me and told me that this was one of her pet peeves. She took the two out of the pile and threw them out. It is hard enough to be taken serious as an actor in the beginning, give yourself a leg up and come in representing yourself as professionally as you can.

BONUS HINT:

Make sure you have at least 2 headshots/resumes that are:

- 8X10s make sure you hand in a headshot that is cut to industry standards 8 inches by 10 inches. I have seen people use photocopies of their headshots and leave them at the regular paper size of 8.5X11 inches. To many this says that you are lazy.
- Cut the resume down to 8X10 to fit.
- Make sure your headshot is *stapled* to your resume.
- Make sure the picture looks like you, and that it is current. You might have a ton of old headshots, I do. Be professional and give them the most current one that you have.
- Not wrinkled or stained. I know you would think this goes without saying but I've seen some gnarly looking eight by tens.

THE WAITING ROOM

Okay we are now getting closer to the room. The waiting room at a Casting Director's office is a strange animal. You will get to know some of the people in there if you don't already. I find that you will always see some of the usual suspects, plus a couple new faces from time to time. There is so much energy in that room both good and bad. There's a sense of hope... at least there should be- if not, why walk in there at all.

There is competition. Everyone sizes each other up. There may even be someone there who wishes you were not there. Your job is to sign in and wait for your turn. Make sure you sign in and out. Sometimes there is a lot of socializing in the waiting room, and depending on the weight of the part, I like to socialize myself, these are our peers after all. There is always some work talk as that is usually the biggest thing we have in common. You may find that when the part is heavier you will want to keep to yourself and so will most of the other people. So if you feel the need to keep to yourself then do so.

I was going in for a very dark part; I was going to play an ex-con who had just killed a man's wife in front of him. The ex-con used a knife to stab the woman to death while forcing her husband to watch. I usually don't go into the room in character but I did for this one. I even carried a small knife with me into the audition. (I don't suggest you do this… ever.) No one could see it was on me, but I knew it was there. I didn't speak to anyone and to make sure no one spoke to me I listened to music while I waited. My music of choice was loud heavy metal to set the tone.

If you do socialize, remember to be as quiet as possible, there is an actor in that room that is trying to do the best job possible. When you get in the room you will not want to be distracted by someone's laugh from the waiting room so it is only fair that you be as quiet as possible while you wait for your turn.

Most importantly, be nice to the person that signs you in if there is one. This is the gatekeeper for the Casting Director and will let them know if you were rude or unprofessional. Also remember, the Casting Assistant of today is the Casting Director of tomorrow.

THE ROOM

When you walk in the room, *walk in the room*. This may be the very first time these people see you. First impressions are very important. Be nice, be polite and be confident. Walk with purpose and take your time. I feel that walking in the room is as important as the audition itself.

Consider the panel as your allies, this will help with your nerves. An important thing to keep in mind is that they want you to be great as much, if not more than you want to be. They need to cast that part and they need to give it to someone who can do the job. I look at this part of the audition as the "show them ME." I will walk in confident, because in the back of my head I know that the people in front of me have a problem, they need to cast this part, and I can solve that problem for them. Everyone in that room is nervous but you have to be the least nervous person in the room.

When I walk in I try to portray an air of confidence that tells everyone in the room, "Relax everybody, I'm here and I won't let you down." If it helps, say it in your head as you walk in, I do. Look everyone in the eye as you walk in and go to the mark on the floor. The <u>mark</u> on the floor will most likely be an X or a T taped on the floor. The camera and their seating have been arranged with this mark in mind. Say hello and smile, this is where some pleasantries are exchanged.

I usually don't like to go in the room in character so I can let the people in the room see my personality. At the end of the day if given the choice between two actors equal in every way but one is nice and polite, and the other one is not so personable, who do you think they will want to spend a 12-hour day with?

I try not to initiate a handshake, remember that these people are going to see a large number of people that day and that's a lot of germs. So don't offer a handshake, but do not decline one if it's extended.

So at this point you will be standing on your mark. You're in the middle of the room. You are the center of attention consider it **your** room and **your** time, use it. If you need to sit for your read, then sit. Let the camera operator know if you will be moving around so he or she can follow you. If you want to walk into the **frame,** let them know that you want to step out and then into the frame. When I say step out I mean out of the camera frame, do not leave the room. That being said, be prepared to stand if there is no chair or if they absolutely want you to stand for whatever reason. *Be ready for anything.* You never know what they can throw at you in that room. Don't let the things they do affect your read. If they are mean to you, or short with you just eat it and move on with your read. Keep in mind that these people might have been in the room auditioning people for hours and may be tired, hungry, grumpy or just having a bad day. It is up to you to be professional and do your job.

You will be asked if you have any questions and if you do, ask them. If you don't have any questions say no and get ready to start. If they don't ask you and you do have a question let them know and ask your question.

THE SLATE

To most, this part will appear to be simple but it is important. Not everyone knows how to do this part. The casting director will ask you to slate before your audition. You will state your name and your agency and the part that you are reading for. If you don't have an agent, give your contact information. Some people like to slate in character, I don't. I try to portray my friendly "you will love working with me" side. You may be asked to show your profiles, if you are then do quarter turns and let them tell you when to move. This shows them how you look from different sides.

THE READ

When the time comes to start the audition take a second or two to get into your zone, to get into character, get your mojo going, get psyched, do what ever you do to get ready because it's game time. Make sure that you establish a connection with your reader. Forget that anyone else is in the room, just focus on the scene, your reader and that moment. From time to time there will be some distractions in the room, whether it is noise from the actors outside or someone in the room texting or flipping pages in the script or looking at other head-shots. That last one sucks, I had it happen once when I was in the middle of a reading and I noticed one of the producers had picked up someone else's headshot. There is no knowing what is going on in their minds, so don't let it bring you out of the moment.

A little thing that I learned a while ago was not to staple the sides together but instead of turning the page over behind the rest of the sides I would keep them loose and shuffle the page back. I find that this is a much smaller movement and will be less distracting to you and to the people watching you audition.

If you are not going to be off page, which I strongly suggest that you are, I would say you should at least have the first couple lines off page so you can establish a connection with your reader. Make eye contact with the reader and listen to what they are saying to you, you can't do this if you are looking down at a sheet of paper. This is most helpful when you are going in for a cold read and you haven't had time to memorize the sides. I would also suggest knowing what your last line is too so that you can leave off the scene with a strong connection to your reader.

I like to improvise from time to time… who am I kidding, I do it every chance I get. I like to add a **button** at the end of the read if I don't have the last line. **Not everyone likes this so improvise at your own risk. There is a big difference between TV, film and commercial auditions. In my experience there is much less opportunity to improvise in TV auditions, as they are usually pretty tight on the script. I find that you can play a little more in film auditions. When there is copy (lines) in a commercial they were very carefully put there and they offer the least amount of Improv opportunity, since they only have 30 seconds to get their message through.

If they ask you to do it again, be happy; it is a good thing.

I love it when the director is in the room and gives me direction, this is a test not only to see what kind of chops you have but also how well you take directions. This is when you wow them with how prepared you are with the material and just how great an actor you are.

One of my favorite audition moments was the time I was going out for a series regular for a new NBC show. I had already been to four auditions for this character; I would say there were maybe 20 of us when we started. After every audition they cut some guys out. At this point there were just four of us left and we were waiting in the hallway for the casting director to open the office door. All along the walls of the hallway were framed posters of all the previous and current NBC shows. I saw the casting director's assistant walking towards us and as she unlocked the doors she said, "At some point all of the people in those posters were where you are now." I know that was a great moment in itself, but that wasn't quite my favorite….

19

Later on in the room it was just the director and the casting director sitting behind a huge conference table. I walked in and said hello. We got started right away. I did my thing. He said it was good but he wanted to try something different. He told me to play the scene as if I was the "class clown." I did. He said it was good again, with a smile on his face. He gave me one more note. He said to play the character like he was "The Man" in the team. He said that everyone is counting on me to "get shit done." I took a second. I did up one more button and straightened my shirt, I walked into the frame with poise and confidence I've been talking about. And I did my thing. When I was done the director slapped the desk and said, "That was a great f*&king transition." He said thank you, stood up and shook my hand. This audition led to me **testing** for the network, we were now down to two of us. I did not end up getting the part, but this is still one of my favorite moments. Even though I didn't get it I made a great impression on the CD who remembered me down the road.

I found out later on that they went **local** with the character. The show was shooting in Hawaii and they hired an actor that lives there. This goes to show you that you never know why they choose who they choose for the part. All you can do is be prepared and do the best job you can and…

Leave it all in the room.

Once you are done make sure to thank everyone and leave. And sign out.

You are done.

THE HARD PART

Now the hard part begins. Get it all out of your head. Chances are that you will come up with a great way of playing the scene when you leave the audition, but *let it go*. Now it's a waiting game. I like to keep track of my auditions so I write them down on an audition log (which you can get from dancingsumo.com/intheroom) as soon as I can, and leave a comment on the comment area of the tracking sheet. There are several reasons why I like to log my auditions.

1. Keeps track of whom I am reading for.

2. When I get a call back I like to see what I wore to the audition.

3. I like to track the number of auditions my agent gets me.

4. I like tracking the number of auditions I have compared to bookings.

I like to remind myself that...

Auditions are about selection not rejection.

If I don't get the part it was simply that they went with someone else, it wasn't that I was so terrible that they rejected me personally. In reality only they will know why they chose the way they did. But, don't let it get you down. You could have been a better actor than the person they went with but maybe you remind the director of the guy who stole his high school sweetheart, or remind the producer of her the high school sweetheart. Either way, they may not want to look at you for 12 hours a day while shooting....but that has everything to do with them, not you.

There is a lot of work that I put into auditioning but *it is the job*. I believe that auditioning is the work part of the job. I like to think that getting to be on set is the reward for all the work that goes into preparing not only the audition for that part, but also all the auditions that I didn't book.

Fade To Black

ADIOS

I personally love to audition because I know that, that day I got to *act*.

I leave you with a cheer that one of my favorite directors would always say as he lifted his glass... "I wish you Salud, Dinero y Amor." (Health, Money and Love)

Thank you for reading my words and remember to have fun doing all of this. We are lucky, very lucky to be able to do what we do.

I am grateful to be an actor and I hope you are too.

Break a leg.

GLOSSARY OF TERMS

Biz   Show business.

Breakdown   Casting directors put out a call for submissions for
                   every project they cast. They use a form that gives
                   the agents information about the character it includes
                   the name of the project the people involved a brief
                   synopsis of the move and a character description for
                   all the parts being cast.

Character   The part that you will be playing in the show.

Chops   The technical skill of an artist.

Frame   What the camera sees without moving the lens.

Local   When a show shoots in a location outside of Los
                   Angeles they will hire people who live in that city to
                   save money on flights and accommodations.

Mark   A spot on the floor where the casting people want
                   you stand . This depends on where the camera, lights
                   and any sound equipment are set up.

Off Page   Being off page is to have the lines memorized so you
                   don't have to look at the page.

Pilot   A pilot or pilot episode of a TV show is the very first
                   complete episode that a creator or producer will show
                   to network executives in Hollywood, trying to sell an

entire series to that network.

Series Regular A character in a show that appears on every episode.

Sides The pages of the script that the character you are auditioning for appears in.

Testing The final audition for a network show. They might put you on camera to see how you look and work with other cast members. These are usually very stressful since there are a lot of people in the room with you. There will usually some network executives to watch you.

The Read The audition.

The Room Simply the audition room.

The Work All the techniques that you have learned in preparing the character for the project.

www.ingramcontent.com/pod-product-compliance
Lightning Source LLC
Chambersburg PA
CBHW060644030426
42337CB00018B/3436